To write,

My poem writing

rebel.

I Love You.

xoxo

Sera

73

Pansy
a collection of poetry

❧

by Andrea Gibson

Write Bloody Publishing
America's Independent Press

Austin, TX

WRITEBLOODY.COM

Gibson, Andrea.
1ˢᵗ edition.
ISBN: 978-1938912559

Cover Designed by Jennifer Heuer and Heather Mann
Author Photo by Maria Del Naja
Proofread by Andie Flores
Edited by Derrick Brown and Andie Flores
Interior Layout by Andie Flores
Type set in Bergamo from www.theleagueofmoveabletype.com

Printed in Tennessee, USA

Write Bloody Publishing
Austin, TX
Support Independent Presses
writebloody.com

To contact the author, send an email to writebloody@gmail.com

MADE IN THE USA

With gratitude for the art and activism of Leslie Feinberg who died of Lyme Disease on November 15, 2014.

"Gender is the poetry each of us makes out of the language we are taught."

"I do not believe that our sexuality, gender expression and bodies can be liberated without making a ferocious mobilization against imperialist war and racism an integral part of our struggle."

-Leslie Feinberg

PANSY

Pansy

ELBOWS

I get panic attacks when I'm being looked at.
I get hungry in crowds.
I eat potato chips to crunch away the noise.

The noise is not noise
if I'm the one who is in control
of the loud.

You can't see me if I close my eyes.
You have no idea where I am.

I guarantee I am somewhere
thinking about the people
who choose the middle seat on an airplane.
When our elbows touch

my heart goes so fast.
I dare myself to not pull away.
It's the point of life,
don't let anyone tell you different.

The point of life is increasing the amount of time
you can get your elbow to stay.

My joy likes to run from my body quick as it can.
I've been practicing holding it
like you'd practice holding your breath
at a public pool.
I can do about half a lap
before my panic freaks out on its little red whistle.

My panic is not a lifeguard,
but you can't tell my panic that.
My panic googled, "How to perform CPR on yourself."

Despite how it might look
I was raised right.

My father is a good man.
When I asked him why
he stayed three years in Vietnam he told me
the army offered him a free trip to France
if he stayed the extra year.
When he left the room
my mother said, *No, Andrea, that's not true.*
Your father stayed the extra year so his brother
wouldn't have to go.

When I came out to my parents
they took me to a psychiatrist to get my head fixed.
The psychiatrist said, *You are not responsible*
for your family's happiness.

But my father's brother is a happy man.
It was a lot to lose.

I never nightmared so much as I did those years.
I was at a Catholic school playing
basketball for the Lady Monks.
I was taking environmental science
from a nun who did not believe in dinosaurs.
What I knew about extinction
was that my family stopped calling

and I started working demolition and volunteered
to run the jack hammer through the asbestos tiles
on the building's floor.

When I finally got my degree
the only job I could find
was as a telemarketer selling a product
called "Score," a cologne "Guaranteed to get
any man laid in the club."
There are times when your life is not on the upswing.

And no one was saying it was gonna get better.

When they said *straighten up*
they meant straighten up.
But some of us can't help but jackknife out of the net.
Some of us know Love

is not the only closet
we will be told never to come out of.
There is also the closet of Grief.
The closet of Sorrow.
The closet of Panic.
Of Terror. Of Rage.
The closet of Awe and Want and Bliss.

The world asked for a stencil,
for the chatter of cordial manufactured machine,
and yet here were are
with all the honest grit
that we feel, daring
our elbows, out-noising the noise,
blowing whistles at the past
for not being the past.

Making no excuses
for wanting to feel too much.

There is no tragedy
that doesn't knock the wind out of us,
but we follow that wind where it goes
running with our wind chimes dragging behind us
like we were just married

to knowing the breakdown
is what trampolines the bouncing back.

I am always a groom
just learning to pull my own weight
without wishing my past weighs less than it does.
Learning Brave

is a hand-me-down suit from Terrified as Hell.

Dress me in whatever will get me
through the door of my heart.

Get my faith in us under your skin.
Hold my stubborn in the palm of your free.
Tell whoever is resting their elbows
beside you tonight,
Thank god you never got braces.
Your bite looks like a city skyline.
I bet you'll leave that kind of mark on the world.

A LETTER TO MY DOG EXPLORING THE HUMAN CONDITION

Dear Squash,
aka Squashy, aka Squishy
aka Squash-A-Rooni-Gibson
aka Squish-Squash-and-Ya-Don't-Stop
aka Miracle Button
aka Little Perfect Peanut
aka My Beating Heart with Fur and Legs,

I know you think it's insane that I still poop in the house,
that I choose to wear underwear and pants
giving no one the opportunity to smell my true disposition,
that on the days I need to feel better about myself
I don't just pee on someone's pee.

Don't worry, I am not fooled by my thumbs.
I know I am not the tadpole's final project.
I know I am not the last species evolution prays to become.
I can't even swallow my own pride
long enough to let myself drool
when something smells delicious.

What must you think of my mirror face?
Or how much of my day I spend practicing
my butch voice? My *Baby, I'll fix your carburetor
with my tool kit* voice. When you know full well
there is nothing in my toolkit

besides a massive collection of self-help books
that have helped me do nothing but
feng shui the skeletons in my closet.

Don't you just love how that femur accents the sofa set, Squash?

I'm sorry I cry every time I take you to the vet.
I'm sorry they take your temperature like that.

I'm sorry I take you there when you've only got a bug bite.
Humans hold on so tight to the leash of life,

but you will roll in anything dead and wear it like perfume.

I wish I had your nose for eternity.
I wish I could see what you see:

why the squirrels satan your eyes,
why the postman deserves to die
even when he's not bringing bills.
What's with hating the shadow
the Peace Lily makes on the floor
of the living room?

I know I let you down every day
I choose to not murder the vacuum.

Is it bad that I refuse to teach you to not be afraid of men?
Is it bad that I want you to keep your bite and your snarl
and your gleaming teeth? Is it bad that when they call you a risk,
I call you a feminist?

You never make fun of your friend Chloe's under-bite,
or your friend Willow's limp, or your friend
Harvey's past trouble with the law.

You never criticize me for being too uptight
to let my hair down. Even though you can
let yours all the way out:
all over my black pants
my black hoodie
the car
the couch
the chair.

The online merch store that sells my books and t-shirts
wrote me a letter saying, *We can't continue to sell your products
if they continue to be covered in so much of your dog's hair.*

I just assumed anything covered in you would increase in value.

Remember when I told that woman I loved her
then whispered in your ear, *You're still my number one girl?*

It's true.

If I could I would put your beating heart in my mouth
and suck on it like a piece of candy
so I could truly understood how
you got so sweet.

I know my therapist likes you more than she likes me
and I still let you sleep on her couch.
You taught me a good nap is the best therapy.
You taught me to sit
when I damn well want to sit.

I don't care that you never talk about
capitalism or patriarchy
or the heteronormative hegemonic paradigm.
I know you're saving the world every time
you get poo stuck in your butt hair
and you don't go looking for someone to blame.

Speaking of looking for someone...
I can't imagine what you think of sex.
I can't tell if you think it's a slobbering
badly-boundaried belly rub
or a poorly-aimed fistfight.
You just perch on the end of the bed
tilting your head back and forth
wondering why I still haven't
taken my pants off.

I have issues, Squash.

Humans have issues.

We dig holes to bury our own hearts.
We chew on our own bones.
We escape the predators but still can't
shake them off. Some of us
wear our own bodies the way
your friend Berlin wore that cone around her head --
so embarrassed.

But I've never had a better teacher
at uncaging my spirit than you.
Never had a better reason to
stop playing dead than that day
I saw your face at the shelter:

your little nose
pressed against the cold glass
staring up at me
like I was a gay Noah's ark.

My heart my heart my heart --
every time I give you a treat
you run around the house looking for a place to hide it
until you finally come to where I'm sitting
and hide it directly under me.

The most important thing I have ever built in my life is your trust.

May you always feel entitled
to more than your fair share of the bed.
May you always tear the stuffing
out of every toy I give you
so I can constantly be reminded

to keep spilling my guts,
to keep saying, *I don't know how
I will ever make peace with
the shortness of your lifespan.*
But I promise to make sure

you know you are so loved
every second you are here. You know
my hands will build the sturdiest ark
they possibly can to hold
your holy howl
and your holy bark
and your holy beg.

Squash-A-Rooni Gibson.
Little Perfect Peanut.
My Beating Heart with Fur and Legs.

THE MADNESS VASE, AKA THE NUTRITIONIST

The nutritionist said I should eat root vegetables.
Said if I could get down 13 turnips each day
I would be grounded, rooted. Said
my head would not keep flying away
to where the darkness lives.

The psychic told me my heart
carries too much weight.
Said for twenty dollars she'd tell me what to do.
I handed her the twenty and she said, *Stop
worrying darling, you will find a good man soon.*

The first psycho-therapist said
I should spend three hours a day
sitting in a dark closet with my eyes closed
and my ears plugged. I tried it once
but couldn't stop thinking about
how gay it was to be sitting in the closet.

The yogi told me to stretch everything but truth.
Said to focus on the out-breath, said everyone
finds happiness if they can care more
about what they give
than what they get.

The pharmacist said, Klonopin, Lamictal,
Lithium, Xanax.

The doctor said an antipsychotic might help me
forget what the trauma said.

The trauma said, *Don't write this poem.*

Nobody wants to hear you cry
about the grief inside your bones.

But my bones said, *Tyler Clementi dove*
into the Hudson River convinced
he was entirely alone.

My bones said, *Write the poem.*

To the lamplight considering the river bed.
To the chandelier of your faith hanging by a thread.
To every day you cannot get out of bed.
To the bullseye of your wrist.

To anyone who has ever wanted to die:

I have been told sometimes the most healing
thing we can do
is remind ourselves over and over and over
Other people feel this too.

The tomorrow that has come and gone
and it has not gotten better. When you are half-finished
writing that letter to your mother that says, *I swear to God I tried,*
but when I thought I'd hit bottom, it started hitting back.

There is no bruise like the bruise loneliness kicks
into your spine. So let me tell you
I know there are days
it looks like the whole world is dancing in the streets
while you break down like the doors of their looted buildings.

You are not alone

in wondering who will be convicted of the crime
of insisting you keep loading your grief
into the chamber of your shame.

You are not weak

just because your heart feels so heavy.

I have never met a heavy heart that wasn't a phone booth
with a red cape inside.

Some people will never understand

the kind of superpower it takes for some people
to just walk outside some days. I know
my smile can look like the gutter of a falling house.
But my hands are always holding tight

to the rip chord of believing
a life can be rich like the soil,

can make food of decay,
turn wound into highway.

Pick me up in a truck with that bumper sticker that says,
"It is no measure of good health
to be well adjusted to a sick society."

I have never trusted anyone
with the pulled back bow of my spine
the way I trust the ones who come undone at the throat
screaming for their pulses to find the fight to pound.

Four nights before Tyler Clementi
jumped from the George Washington bridge
I was sitting in a hotel room in my own town
calculating exactly what I had to swallow
to keep a bottle of sleeping pills down.

What I know about living is the pain
is never just ours.
Every time I hurt I know
the wound is an echo, so I keep listening
for the moment the grief becomes a window,

when I can see what I couldn't see before.
Through the glass of my most battered dream

I watched a dandelion lose its mind in the wind

and when it did, it scattered a thousand seeds.

So the next time I tell you how easily I come out of my skin
don't try to put me back in. Just say, *Here we are*
together at the window, aching for it all
to get better. But knowing there is a chance

our hearts may have only just skinned their knees.
Knowing there is a chance
the worst day might still be coming.
Let me say right now for the record:

I'm still gonna be here
asking this world to dance.
Even if it keeps stepping on my holy feet.

You, you stay here with me, okay?

You stay here with me. Raising
your bite against the bitter dark,
your bright longing
your brilliant fists of loss.

Friend, if the only thing we have to gain in staying
is each other, my god that is plenty.
My god that is enough.

My god, that is so so much for the light to give.
Each of us at each other's backs
whispering over and over and over,

Live. Live. Live.

EXPLORING MY RELATIONSHIP HISTORY

I told the boys in the neighborhood
to line up against the fence
and stand there still as soldiers
while I threw rocks at the terrified targets
of their scrawny bodies.

I said who ever lasted the longest
could marry me. I threw almost all of the rocks
at Johnny and Steve and Tommy,
who I didn't want to marry, and tossed a single
weightless pebble at Malcolm, who I loved.

We held the wedding by the tadpole creek
and Malcolm said, "In sickness and in hell"
because he thought that's how it went, or
possibly, it was specific to me.

EMERGENCY CONTACT

She might be your type.
But I'm the exact font.

I am outside your window.
Throw down your hair.

I mean the hair you pulled from the drain
when you were cleaning your tub.

I want everything you have ever tried to wash away.

The first time you were bullied in junior high.
The last time you blushed from a compliment.
Every fever that hasn't yet broken. It's true,
I have never made a love potion that hasn't blown up,
but your mouth is the sexiest beaker.

Bend me over your periodic table
then try to tell me we don't have chemistry.

Of course I am poly.
As in polygraph machine.
As in I can tell you are lying
when you say don't want me
in a cheerleading outfit
spelling only your name
with pom poms.

Take me to the bullfights.
What is love, if it's not running straight for the bull?
Then putting him on a sailboat bound for an animal sanctuary
in Massachusetts where he'll be forever best friends
with a pig named George.

Love is a downpour of shelter.

I want to wrap you in blankets

until you are so dry you're wet.
I want to come clean in our dirtiest bed.

Fuck playing the field.
Do you know how wild I could grow
in the flower pot beside your desk?

All of your petals are welcome here.
And every ounce of your drought.
I will never ask you to weed your fear.
When I say I want all of you, I mean even
the chair jammed under the doorknob.

I am a master at holding my ear to the wall
and knowing when the coast is clear.

The coast is most clear when there are lovers
making love ignite the lighthouse.

Let every ship come home to harbor.

I promise to be careful
with the bird's nest in the chimney.

You can have all of my pipe organs.
You can make an opera of my throat.

You told me years ago
I have to start writing the poems
I am terrified to write.

Here you go.

I don't care if you break my heart in half.

I just want to have written your name
as my emergency contact.

BIT

I miss the crickets
and the creek
and the blueberry field

that stained my baby teeth.

I miss running
for my life
through the cut grass.

I miss the clotheslines
my grandma's hands
played like a stringed guitar.

I miss the colors
in the church windows,
how it didn't matter
that you couldn't see outside.
I miss sneaking up the stairs
to the steeple to rest
my hands on the gold bell.

I miss believing
in the same thing as everybody else.

My mother
fixing my hair for my school pictures.
Me, fixing my heart
on the rowdy wind.

Every kid I knew
wanted to grow up to be a star.
I did too, but I was afraid of the dark
where the stars lived.

I'd go fishing in the puddle
behind Stevie's house.

I'd tie a gummy worm to a string
that was tied to a stick.
My mother called me home
before anything bit.

In the spirit of attempting a healthy dialogue with people leaving racist comments on my Facebook page. In the spirit of understanding it should never be the responsibility of People of Color to educate white people about white supremacy and white privilege. In the spirit of Leslie Feinberg who said, "I do not believe that our sexuality, gender expression and bodies can be liberated without making a ferocious mobilization against imperialist war and racism an integral part of our struggle." #BlackLivesMatter

A LETTER TO WHITE QUEERS, A LETTER TO MYSELF

Another Black man has been murdered in our streets. And I am white as a ghost haunting my own grief. Thinking, "Who am I to feel grief?"

Thinking, "My god, who am I not to?"

I am writing to tell you about 1998, when Matthew Shepard, a young gay man from Laramie, Wyoming was tied to a fence, beaten with a pistol until his skull cracked, and left for 18 hours in the frozen cold, his face entirely covered in blood except for the places his tears had washed clean.

I am writing to tell you I was in a coffee shop in Seattle holding my love's hand when I heard the news. The grief tsunamied from my eyes immediately down to my knees.

I can still feel how my knees buckled, each one of them, like a bible belt snapping around the neck of an 18-hour scream. On the street outside of the coffee shop I could feel my last bit of unburied faith swallowing the gravel in the dug-out grave of my chest.

I could feel my own mother kissing Matthew's forehead in a hospital where she knew even the doctor's god was rooting for a flatline. For weeks I couldn't look at anyone I loved without imagining hate crushing their spines into a powder that would be snorted at a party after a football game.

Four months prior, James Byrd, Jr., a Black man from Jasper, Texas was chained to the back of a truck, dragged for 3 miles along the concrete, conscious the entire time until his head was severed and his remains were found in 81 separate places along the side of the road.

I am writing to tell you that I do not remember where I was or how I felt when I heard the news. For a lot of our community, 1998 was the year Matthew Shepard died.

I am writing to tell you I have been spending a lot of time thinking, *Who are my people? What determines whose death will storm my chest, will flood my eyes? Will make me want to burn down a city and pray with every ounce of my winded grace that more than smoke will rise?*

Last year, an older gay man in my neighborhood shot himself in his own bed. After his family refused to attend his funeral, refused to collect his belongings, the mattress was hosed off, tossed in the backyard, and his house was foreclosed. I heard a rumor that the house was going to sell for an incredible deal. I immediately imagined flocks of straight people going on and on about how his grave would look fabulous with a granite counter top.

I kept picturing the holiday party they would throw in the "bargain" of his unlivable pain. His life nothing but a stain to them. Nothing but something to scrub out of the rug in the new nursery. I walked by his house for weeks imagining an SUV full of soccer cleats running back and forth over his ghost in the driveway.

I had been up all night imagining what I'd say to whatever thief would have the audacity to rip up his garden and plant Bermuda grass, when I finally said to my friend, *Ya know, I have been writing for 16 years and the word "gentrification" has never made it into a single one of my poems.* Who are my people? Where is my rage when they are stealing Brown and Black people's homes?

I am writing to tell you that last week, someone posted a comment on my Facebook page that said, *You're the kind of bitch it would be a pleasure to hang.* And that was tucked in between thousands of other comments equally as fucked, some of them, like yours, from people in the queer community, who furiously disagreed with a post I wrote about Michael Brown being murdered by a white supremacist system designed to murder the hearts, bodies, and spirits of People of Color.

Something very hard to stomach in this life is the fact that we are all going to learn and grow at a pace that will hurt people, and lately I have been furious with my own pace. Furious that I could be holding the candlestick of a microphone for this many years and have it burn this far down without shining a hell of a lot more light on the truth of what I know white is.

You wanna know what white is? White is having somebody tell you you'd be a pleasure to hang, having a whole lot of people agree, and not even thinking to lock your door that night.

White is knowing if someone is going to be hung you are not the one. White is having all of Eric Garner's air in your lungs. No matter how queer you are. No matter how anything we are. If we are white we have Eric Garner's air in our lungs tonight. And that means our breath is not ours to hold. That means our exhale is owed to mercy, to the riot of our unowned hearts, to the promise that who we weep and fight and tear down the sun for will not only be our own faces in the mirror.

We cannot be married to apathy without wearing the rings of the poplar tree when our country is still lynching and still calling the hung bodies shade. When our country is right now rolling a red carpet from the blood that pours and people are dying for us to notice that our footsteps are red. Our silence is not a plastic gun. It is fully loaded. It has lethal aim.

It is 1998 and James Byrd, Jr. is not yet dead. He is walking from a party to towards his home on the other side of town. And you and I are somewhere. We are somewhere. Pouring what we will pour into the cups of our hearts. Spilling what we will spill, into the screamed open earth.

ANGELS OF THE GET-THROUGH

This year has been the hardest year of your whole life.
So hard you cannot see a future most days.
The pain is bigger than anything else.
Takes up the whole horizon
no matter where you are.

You feel unsafe. You feel unsaved.
Your past so present you can feel your baby teeth.
Sitting on the couch, you swear your feet don't reach the floor.

You keep remembering the first time
you saw a bird's nest held together by an old shoe lace
and the scraps of a plastic bag.

You knew the home of a person
could be built like that.
A lot of things you'd rather throw away.

You keep worrying you're taking up too much space.
I wish you'd let yourself be the Milky Way.

Remember when I told you
I was gonna become a full-time poet,
and you paid my rent for three years?
Best Friend,

angel of the get-through,
all living is storm chasing.
Every good heart has lost its roof.
Let all the walls collapse at your feet.
Scream Timber when they ask you
how you are.

FINE is the suckiest answer.
It is the opposite of *HERE*.

Here is the only place left on the map.

Here is where you learn laughter can go extinct
and come back.

I am already building a museum
for every treasure you unearth in the rock
bottom. Holy vulnerable cliff.
God mason, heart heavier
than all the bricks.
Say this is what the pain made of you:
an open open open road.
An avalanche of *feel it all.*

Don't let anyone ever tell you
you are too much. Or
it has been too long.

Whatever guards the feet
on the bridge of the song,
you are made of that thing.
That unbreakable note.
That photograph
of you at five years old.
The year you ran away from school
because you wanted to go home.
You are almost there.

You are the same compass you have always been.
You are the same friend who never left my side
during my worst year. You caught every tantrum
I threw with your bare hands, chucked it back

at the blood moon, said, *It's ok. Everyone's survival
looks a little bit like death sometimes.*

I wrote a poem called "Say Yes"
while I was cursing your name
for not letting me go.

Best friend, this is what we do.

We gather each other up.
We say, *The cup is half*

yours and half mine. We say,
Alone is the last place you will ever be.

We say, *Tonight let's stay inside*
reading Pema Chödrön
while everyone else is out on the town.

Pema will say, "Only to the extent that we expose ourselves
over and over to annihilation
can that which is indestructible in us be found."

You'll say, *Pema is so wise.*
And I'll say, *Yes she is. And we are too.*

Angels of the get-through.
We are too.

LALALOL

And then came the day
I discovered my mother had been writing "LOL"
on the Facebook walls of her grieving friends.

Roger was a kind man. LOL.
Susan left this world far too soon. LOL.
Heaven has another angel. LOL.

Bless her heart and the hearts of the grieving families
but I couldn't help but Laugh Out Loud.
My poor mother, trying to send "Lots Of Love"
and not knowing how.

I knew if I told her she would never be able to forgive herself.
But I knew if I didn't...

Jenny will be deeply missed. LOL.
You will meet again in a better place. LOL.
I'm so so sorry to hear about your loss. LOL.

What do we owe to the truth?
Certainly not our mothers' smiles.

I couldn't think of a worse thing to take from someone
than the comfort they had offered others.

So I stayed quiet, and prayed that if she became
the laughing stock of town, the laughers would
Laugh Out Loud and she would hear it the way she always had.
Just Lots Of Love. Just Lots And Lots And Lots Of Love.

TO THE MEN CATCALLING MY GIRLFRIEND WHILE I'M WALKING BESIDE HER

One of the biggest perks to looking the way I do
is that I virtually never have to listen
to someone like you
verbally suck your own dick,
while telling yourself
I am what you're swallowing.

How do you not know that when you open your mouth
like that, women imagine your OKCupid photo
as a mugshot? Fail.
Fail is what you do

every time you think you can
ace manhood without ever
showing up to class. I mean class
as in decency, as in common courtesy,
as in the opposite of

Let me get a look at that ass, Baby Doll!

Congratulations on being another dude
who got his catcalls from *Toys R Us*.
You unoriginal hand-me-down of mediocrity.
You mosquito

biting your own balls in a swamp
of your mother's regret. Yes, I know
it's low to call even assholes names.
But any feminist who has ever taken
the high road will tell you

the high road gets backed up, and sometimes
we need to take a detour straight through
the belly of uncensored rage.

Sometimes we get tired

of "seeing people's humanity" when they
are outright refusing to show us
their humanity. And so far
all you've shown me is that

your voice box is a Rubix Cube
you couldn't get right even if
you peeled the fucking stickers off.

You do not own the air.

Not everyone takes a bullet
as a compliment. And yes,
even a *Hey Baby* can spiral
like a bullet if it is aimed

at someone who is not, in fact, your baby.

If women have to play dead to walk by
your doorstep, you might want to
do some work on why a casket
turns you on.

You might want to do some work
on why her flinch and startle makes you think
you are in charge more than it makes
you realize your own power outage.
This world is dark with men blowing themselves

out. Men burying their own spines
in the weight of what they think is theirs
to take, to own, to muzzle, to drag
into the ditch. Men who don't get

what they want then shout the word Bitch
across the street like they're two years old
throwing a tantrum with their baby diapers on.

Like they think their dick is the golden ticket

at the Willy Wonka factory and they can't imagine
anyone would have an intolerance to *Hey Sugar*
so they call you a *Slut* or a *Whore* or a *Dyke*.

Congratulations, you got the last one right.

Somebody get him a tote bag.
Somebody get some construction paper
and make him a certificate. Somebody get him
something quick before he feels inadequate

all over a Santa Barbara sorority house.
Before he lines up women like pretty glass bottles
and starts shooting off more than his mouth.

Seriously, if you think you are any different
from a boy who would write a manifesto
to do everything in his power to destroy
everything he cannot have, then prove it

by being the kind of man who isn't killing
time watching his own dignity play dead.
Whose heartbeat doesn't quicken
with the quickening of a woman's footsteps.
Who has enough self respect to not hang himself

out the window of his car, spewing his entitlement.

It is not Rubix Cube hard to keep your mouth shut.
You can do it. You can do it.

THINGS THAT DON'T SUCK

Salamanders. Rotary phones. Super Woman capes. Hopscotch chalk. Unicycles. Hiccups while kissing. Pole Vaults. Gumball machines. Leprechauns. Music Boxes. Welcome mats. Hand-me-down lockets. Train rides. Carnivals. Record players. Sewing kits. Barbershop chairs. Bubbles. Chestnuts. Barnacle hugs. Door frames. Melted crayons. Soldiers in the airport on their way home. Icicles. Time capsules. Hourglasses. Recess bells. Thrift store coffee mugs. Lost and found boxes. Go-Carts. Tambourines. Fire pits. Paper boats. Snap peas. Snowflakes. Bay windows. Porch swings. Dance routines. Macaroni necklaces. Flying ladybugs. High fives. Ferris wheels. Extra buttons. Crooked teeth. Dust drawings. Bearded women. Fabric stores. Turtle faces. Sleepovers. Mixed Tapes. Grandmothers. Freckles. Lily pads. Farmers' tans. Windpipes. Accordions. Anyone willing to play the shakers in a band. The day I was so in love I mistook a nuclear power plant for a lighthouse. French kisses. The smell of a dog's paw. Thumb wars. Letters in the mailbox. The things we never ordered but still arrived. Riding in the back of a pick-up truck beneath a holy New England sky. Banjo strings. Best friends. Tutus on boys. Tutus on girls. Hummingbirds. Whittle sticks. Hail collections. Rocking chairs. Thimbles. Love notes. Cigar boxes. Screen doors. Clawfoot tubs. Hopechests. Skateboard parks. Mismatched socks. Airplane sky-writing proposals. Baby giraffes. Beaver teeth. Porch lights. Tiny houses. Tire swings. Dandelion snow. Drive-in movie dates. Bathrooms without scales. Shitty poems. Chugging calming tea. Sex with the lights on. Sex with the lights off. Basketball hoops in dirt driveways in Iowa. Snort laughs. Sexy Librarians. Vegan chocolate chip cookies. Boomboxes in the car when the stereo breaks. Slip N' Slides. Butterflies that remember being caterpillars. Staying alive.

ROYAL HEART
With thanks to Carolyn Suslovich

You will never be let down by anyone
more than you will be let down by the one
you love the most.

That's how gravity works.
You don't stand in love. You fall.
Further every season.
That's why the truth is harder to tell
every year you have more to lose.

But you can bury your past
in the garden by the tulips.
Water it till it is so alive
it blooms open and lets you go

and you belong to yourself again.

When you belong to yourself again
remember forgiveness
is not a tidy grave.
It is a ready loyal knight
kneeling before your royal heart.

Call in your royal heart -- tell it
bravery can never be measured by a lack of fear.
It takes guts to tremble.

It takes so much tremble to love --
every first date is a fucking earthquake.

Sweet heart, on our first date
I showed off all my therapy.
I flaunted the couch where
I finally sweat out my history.
I pulled out the photo album
from the last time I wore a lie

to the school dance. I smiled and said,
That was never my style.

Look how fixed I am. Look how
there is no more drywall on my fist.
*Look how my wrist is no longer
something I have to hide,* I said,
while I was hiding it.

The telephone pole still down from the storm.

By our third date I'd fixed the line.
I said, *Listen...*
      I have a hard time.
      I cry as often as most people pee.
      And I don't shut the door behind me.
      I'll be up in your face screaming *Seattle
      is too rainy. Seattle is too rainy!
      I'm never gonna be able to live here!*
      I sobbed.

On our 4th date.
I said,
I can't live here, in my body.
I can't live in my body all the time.
It feels too much.

So if I ever feel far away
know I am not gone.
I am just underneath my grief
adjusting the dial on my radio faith
so I can take this life with all of its love
and all of its loss.

I already know you are the place
I'm finally gonna sing without any static.
I'm never gonna wait that extra twenty minutes
to call you back.

And I'm never gonna play hard to get
when I know your life
has been hard enough already.

Everyone's life has been hard
enough already. It's hard to watch,
this game we make of love, like everyone's
playing chess with their scars, saying *Checkmate*
whenever they get out without a broken heart.

Just to be clear, I don't want to get out
without a broken heart.

I intend to leave this life so shattered
there's gonna have to be a thousand separate heavens
for all my separate parts. Can you see how you
bring all the heavens together, to make me whole?
Can you hear god at the gate saying, *Good job...*
You're finally not full of bullshit.

Sweet heart,
I can see the hill before us.
I used to love in one gear.

I don't want a single speed bike
if I can't make it up the hill. I know
exactly how many gears I'm gonna need
to love you well.

You've finally met someone
who is gonna flatten your kneecaps
into skipping stones.

Come do the same to me.
Throw me. Throw me as far as I can go.
I don't want to leave this life
without ever having come home.
And I want to come home to you.

I can figure out the rain.

AN INSIDER'S GUIDE ON HOW TO BE SICK

Never say the words, *This is not my life.*
This pain that wakes you screaming
into the muzzle of the night. That woke
your lover, chased her to another room,
to another life.

This fevered fainting.
This tremoring chest.
The lungs like a mangled kite.
This panic like a cave of bats.

This nurse drawing blood wearing
doubled gloves. This insurance
doesn't cover that. This hurried paycheck
of a doctor after doctor after doctor.

This stethoscope that never hears.
This savior prescription with side effects
worse than the disease. This hospital bed
with fluorescent dark. This *please*
let me have one month when I read more poems
than warning labels.

This not knowing what the tests will say.
This pray pray pray. This airplane's
medical emergency landing.
This shame when you can't walk. *Shame
when you can't fuck.* Shame when
you're home alone sobbing
on another Friday night.

Say, *This is my life.*
This is my precious life.
This is how badly I want to live.

Say, sometimes you have to keep
pulling yourself up by the whip.

Take punch after punch
to the *face-forward*, to the *head-up*
and still uncurl the fist of your grief
like a warm blanket on the cool earth
of your faith. Say, every waiting room

is the kiln where you will finally take shape
to fit into the keyhole of your own gritty heart.
To open mercy. To open your siren throat. Say,
every fever is a love note to remind you
there are better things to be than cool.

Fuck cool. Fuck every pair of skinny jeans
from the month your muscles started atrophying
to a size two. Say *fuck you* to everyone who asks you
if you eat enough. Say *how do you not know*
that is so fucking rude. *Remember*

you never have an obligation to quiet
the tornado in your chest, especially
on a day when another healthy person
claims *you would feel so much better if*
you would just focus your breath

into a Buddha beam of light. Like that light
might miraculously dissolve the knife
that's been churning in your kidneys
for the last six fucking months. Say,

Sunshine please, go back to your job
at the aromatherapy aisle at Whole Foods,
and *leave me alone.* I know how to talk to god,
and right now god does not expect me
to use my inside voice. God knows how
god damn hard I am working to become
a smooth stone so I can skip

on my back across this red red sea.
So I can trust deep in my screaming
bones everything is a lesson. Lesson
number one through infinity:

You will never have a greater opportunity
to learn to love your enemy
then when your enemy
is your own red blood. *Truce*
is a word made of velvet.
Wear it everywhere you go.

PANIC BUTTON COLLECTOR

I get online 30 times a day
for the sole purpose of making sure
I have not accidentally posted a nude photo of myself.

I re-read my emails 14 times before pressing send
to ensure I have not written something in the email
that could convict me of a crime.

Before taking the stage
when asked if I allow flash photography
I always want to say NO
because I'm terrified flash photography will give me epilepsy.
I know it doesn't work like that. Still
I never eat nuts on an airplane
out of fear that I will suddenly develop a nut allergy
and if I have to asphyxiate
I don't want it to happen at 30 thousand feet.

Twice in the last 2 years
I've been de-boarded from a plane
for running screaming down the aisle
as the plane was taking off.

I can't walk through San Francisco without being terrified that
my indigestion is the beginning of an earthquake.
I brace for tsunamis beside lakes in Colorado. I'm not joking.

Every time I see Niagara Falls - I can't take it.
It is too much much.
I have to plug my ears to look at it
I have to close my eyes to listen. Generally,
I can't do all of my senses at the same time.
They are too much much.

For instance, if you touch me without warning,
whoever you are, it will take everything I have
to not hate you.

Imagine your fingers are electrical sockets
and I am constantly aware that I am 70 percent water.

It's not that I've not tried to build a dam.
Ask my therapist who pays her mortgage.
My cost of living went up at 5 years old
when I told my mother, *I have to stop*
going to birthday parties because
every time I hear a balloon pop
I feel like I'm being murdered in the heart.

Last year a balloon popped on the stage where I was performing.
I started crying in front of the whole crowd.
I plugged my ears and kept repeating the word,
Loud, Loud, Loud.

It was super sexy.

That's what I do...I do super sexy.
Like when I ask the super cute barista 11 times,
Are you sure this is decaffeinated?
Are you sure this is decaffeinated?
Are you sure...

Yes, I drink decaffeinated and still jitter like a bug
running from the bright bright bright.

I once spent 4 years of my life
wearing a tight rubber band
hidden beneath my hair
so my brain could have a hug.

When no one's looking
I wear a fuzzy fitted winter hat
that buttons tight beneath the chin,
and I only ever wear a tie
so when I convince myself I'm choking
my senses have something they are certain

they can blame.

As a kid I was so certain I would die
by way of meteor falling on my head
I'd go whole weeks without looking at the sky
because I didn't want to witness the coming of my own death.

I started tapping the kitchen sink 7 times to build a shield.
My mother started making a list
of everything I thought might kill me
in hopes that if I saw my fears they would disappear.

Bless her puddled worry,
but the first time I saw that list
I started filling salad bowls with bleach
and soaking my shoelaces overnight
so in the morning when I ironed them
they would be so white
I'd be certain I had control

of how much dark could break into my life,
how much jackhammer could break into my chest.
But my spine has always been a lasso
that can never catch my breath.

I honestly cannot imagine how it would feel
to walk into a room full of people
and not feel the roof collapsing on my *No No No.*

NO, I am not *fine.*
That word never tells the truth,
and more than anything
I have ever been afraid of
I am terrified of lies:

how they war the world,
how they sound bite our tongues,
how they bone dry the marrow,
how they never out-loud the inside.

How did they let us go through high school
without teaching us Dr. King
spent two decades having panic attacks,
avoided windows, jumped at thunder?

I think we are all part shaking in the storm
part fight the flight,
part run for your life,

part *please like like like like like* me,
part can't breathe. Part scared
to say you're scared. Part say it anyway.
You panic button collector.
You clock of beautiful tics.
You can always always shake like a leaf
on my family tree and know
you belong here.
You absolutely belong here.
And everything you feel is ok.
Everything you feel is ok.

UPON DISCOVERING MY THERAPIST WILLINGLY SHARES AN OFFICE SPACE WITH A MALE THERAPIST WHO IS AN ACCUSED SEX OFFENDER SUPPOSEDLY RECOVERED FROM HIS URGE TO RAPE 13-YEAR-OLD GIRLS

I sat on her couch,
back stiff as a roofied drink,
jaw tight as a tourniquet,
asked if she had forgotten
that I too had been exactly 13,

had only just started my period, was terrified
to use tampons for fear one would get lost inside of me
when the man as old as my father got lost inside of me,
reminded her

that I was yet to find the string of him
anywhere but roped around my own neck.

*I absolutely hear you, she said, But how could I do this work
if I didn't believe in everybody's ability to heal?
In everybody's ability to heal…*

It was a reasonable question
but I could have slit that questions mark's throat.

Kept flashing to the night at the hospital
after I tried to excavate his smirk from my skin,
how I still nightmare the wound bleeding in spurts
like someone trying to hold their laughter in.

Thirteen can be destroyed by a pimple, by a curfew
a half hour earlier than a friend's. I was yet to watch

an R-rated movie without blushing
into the sleeve of my sleepover pajamas
when he X'd out all that was left of the girl in me,
my voice 3 octaves lower by the time he was done.

If you're going to tell me that everyone has the ability to heal,
that everyone has the ability to recover,
then I'm going to ask why I am still covered

in so much shame I rarely go a day without butchering
my own name? Why I can still take a punch
better than I can take a compliment?
Why I teeter so constantly between flight and fight
it's like I'm trying to beat the daylight
out of my own fucking sky,
like my body will never stop fighting him off.

Do you understand how certain I am
that I could have torn my nails into his wrist
pulled out his pulse
deactivating a bomb?

I could have called that peace.
I could have called that not checking my window
a hundred fucking times every single night
before I fall asleep.

What if I don't want the monster
to stop being a monster?

What if that's the only anchor I have left?
What if my sanity depends on being able to point
at the bad thing and say, *That is the bad thing.*

Haven't I already lost enough time
losing track of who the enemy is?
I've spent half of my life not knowing the difference

between killing myself and fighting back.

What if I don't want healing
as much as I want justice?
What if I don't care if justice
looks exactly like revenge?
Do you think I don't know that I can't
want revenge without strapping the bomb
to my own chest?

That's how the dominoes of trauma fall.
You become just another thing about to detonate.

And whatever part of me that could believe in healing
was the part he stole.

So go ask him for my forgiveness. Go ask him.

FERGUSON

A sea of blood, America,
and not even a shell held to your ear.

PANSIES

In my palms
300 broken windows,
glass covering the floor, and amazing light
shining through me.

In my pulse
a pillow fight,
feathers flying everywhere.
I can't stop crying for all those birds.
I can't stop crying.

I plant my fear in the raised bed
in your bedroom.
Pansies bloom all night.

You call me pretty and I don't flinch.
I know I can still be your boyfriend
and tell you, *My grandmother sewed my prom dress
stitch by stitch with her own hands.
The finest suit could not have made me*

more proud.

My want pounds so loud
the neighbors think we're fucking
when I'm just trying to find the nerve
to touch your face. You don't ask god
how long this will last. I don't care
about any of the words on the map
besides YOU ARE HERE.

You are here listening
to me tell you I've been stung by a bee
twice in my life.
Both times on the mouth.
I still carry the stingers under my tongue
so I never forget where honey comes from.

Sweet Sweet Siren,
I imagine you ruining Oklahoma farm boys
in the beds of their daddies' trucks
and I want to take you to church,
show you what I could do to your
confession booth on Saturday night.

You already know
how many poems I have written
to women who were not you.
You already know every word was true.

There is still a tandem bicycle in my garage
I will never be able to ride or sell,
so I know you know I'm not wondering
why you kept your married name.

I AM HERE
watching you do your laundry
and I want to match your socks,
just so you can put them on
and I can take them off.
Take everything off.

Yes, I have a history of fainting.
No, I wasn't lying
when I said,

I'm gonna be more difficult
than anyone you have ever dated.

It's been years since my life was a picnic
where I wasn't freaking out
about the possible gluten allergies of pigeons
being fed bread in the park.

But you will always feel safe
in knowing I will never

make a piñata of your heart.

You will never have to lose yourself
to win me over.

Tell me you're a liar
and I will tell you, *I already know*
you are a master yogi
when it comes to stretching the truth
but I'd be willing to bet we both
have a history of downward dog.
And sometimes you've gotta bend to see god
isn't always clean as a whistle,

but that train is something I can worship,
if only because it keeps showing up.

I am at your station, saying, *If I were a painter*
I would paint all the billboards in your city bright white,
buy a projector, and take you
to a new drive-in movie every single night.

If I were an oven mitt
I'd say, *Don't touch anything hot*
without me.

I'm gonna do stupid things.
I sold my saxophone to help pay for college.
I once smashed a violin to bits.

On our 2nd date, when I said, *So…your vagina,*
it's really rad that babies have come out of it,

what I meant to say is, *Holy god, you've given birth…*
and I can't imagine anything sexier
than a woman checking her children's homework.

For the record, you're getting straight A's in chemistry class.
For the record, I'm flunking math.

It's been too few days to add up to me thinking: Yes,

I'm gonna permanently fuck up your lipstick.
Yes, I'm gonna throw tantrums through your tidy heart.
Yes, I'm gonna fall apart at your mother's dinner table
over spinach and lentils and somebody's sensible doubt.

Yes, I'm gonna run you a bath.
That is to say...I'm gonna run into the rain
over and over with an empty glass
till you are soaking in the certainty
that nothing falls in vain.

Wherever we land
there will always be This Day.
This Day we turn off that song
of my sadness and your shame.

This Day I stop asking
what all the crying is about.
All I know is my name
could rust entirely away
in your perfect mouth.

A GENDERFUL PEP-TALK FOR MY YOUNGER SELF

They want you thinking you're bad at being a girl
instead of thinking
you're good at being yourself.

They want you to buy your blush from a store
instead of letting it bloom
from your butterflies.

They're telling you to blend in,
like you've never seen how a blender works,
like they think you've never seen the mess from the blade.

You're wondering
if you can get a job called
"Going into Labor."

You're wondering
if this world will ever be living proof
of the living.

This world,
that wants you thinking your face is a fashion mistake,
hoping you'll never show up to the ball of your fist.

I need to tell you that someday you will hit
the road with your bow tie and suspenders and
pockets full of pansies.

Someday you will tell a preacher in Colorado that you have two souls
in your shoes so you can Step Up whenever anybody wants you to
worship a god who will walk all over you then call your body water.

Someday your middle finger will be a candle
lit for anyone who tries to rinse
the burning song out of your mouth.

You, the guest of honor, in your own skin.
Your heart: the law, you will break over and over
to let the light in.

Your body, not theirs.
Your spirit, not theirs.
Yours.

Your life, your fury, your compass,
your steel floating in the water, your water
to break in the streets.

ETIQUETTE LEASH

I want to drink punch with
a million genderqueer school kids
taking free martial arts lessons
to survive recess.

I stopped calling myself a pacifist
when I heard Gandhi told women
they should not physically fight off their rapists.

I believe there is such a thing as a non-violent fist.
I believe the earth is a woman muzzled, beaten,
tied to the coal slinging tracks.

I believe the muzzled have every right
to rip off the bible belt
and take it to the patriarchy's ass.

I know these words are gonna get me in trouble.
It is never polite to throw back the tear gas.

Just like it's never polite to bring enough life rafts...
they crowd the balconies where the wealthy shine their jewels.
But sometimes love...sometimes REAL love...is rude.

Is stopping a wedding mid-vow,
just as the bride is about to cry,
to stand up in your pew
to say, *Is everyone here clear
on how diamonds are mined?*

Hallelujah to every drag queen at Stonewall
who made weapons out of her stiletto shoes.

To every activist who's ever stood in the snow
outside of the circus holding a 10-foot photograph
of a baby elephant in chains when it was likely
some little kid's birthday. Hallelujah

to making everyone uncomfortable.
To the terrible manners of truth.
To refusing to clean the blood off the plate.
To knowing love readies its hearts' teeth,

chews through the etiquette leash,
takes down the cell phone tower
after a million people die in wars in the Congo
fighting for the minerals that make cell phones.

Love blows up the dam,

chains itself to the redwood tree,
to the Capitol building,
when a trailer of Mexican immigrants
are found dead on a south Texas roadside.

Love insists well-intentioned white people officially
stop calling themselves color blind,

insists Hope lace its boots,
refuses to be a welcome mat
where hate wipes its feet.

Love asks questions at the most inappropriate times,
overturns the Defense of Marriage Act
then walks the pride parade asking
when the plight of poor single mothers
will ignite our hearts into action like that.

Love is not polite,
deadlocks rush hour traffic
with a hundred stubborn screaming bikes.

Hallelujah to every suffrage movement hunger strike.
Hallelujah to insisting they get your pronouns right.

Hallelujah to tact never winning our spines,

to taking our power all the way back
to the first glacier that had to learn how to swim.

To not turning our heads from a single ugly truth.
To knowing we live in a time
when beauty recruits its models
outside the doors of eating disorder clinics.
That is not a metaphor.

An Indian farmer walks into a crowd of people
and stabs himself in the chest to protest
the poisoning of his land.

A Buddhist monk burns himself alive
on the crowded streets of Saigon.

A U.S. soldier hangs himself
wearing his enemy's dog tags
around his forgotten neck.

May my heart be as heavy as a tuba
in the front row of the Mardi Gras parade
5 months after Katrina.

May it weigh the weight of the world
so I might sweat as much as I cry.

So I might press into the clay
of our precious lives a window,
might our grace riot
the walls down.

May the drought howl us awake.
May we rush into the streets
to do the work of opening
each other's eyes.

May our good hearts
forever be too loud
to let the neighbors sleep.

ON BEING THE BLOW JOB QUEEN OF MY HIGH SCHOOL

There are
a thousand ways

to stay in the closet.
All of them suck.

PARTY

I was 13 the first time
I drank so much the bugs stopped.

A high school party
at Chrissy Olden's house,
a senior, whose mom worked overnights
at the truck stop and embarrassed the customers
by not being embarrassed to lose
a solid 10 minutes
rambling over the register
about who wrote what in her yearbook
in 1971.

I was sitting in the middle
of the living room
on a corduroy couch
telling Katie Mathews,
the only other 8th grader there,
something about the temperature of music.

Somewhere there was a DJ
holding his finger under the faucet
of the party.

Every few minutes
I'd be handed a bottle of something
that razored my tonsils all the way down.
If someone had told me
it was nail polish remover
I would have believed them
but I would not have stopped drinking
the red off of my heart.

Do you remember
the first time you knew you
were absolutely safe?

I stumbled into the bathroom
and locked the door behind me
so I could smile as wide as I had to
without anybody knowing I had to.

The mirror was caked with Aqua Net.
There was enough hair in the sink
to mistake the drain for a pet.

The last person who had vomited
in the toilet had missed the toilet.

A year prior, just before my grandfather
swallowed the worm of his life,
he leaned his yellow face into my terrified eyes
and made me promise to *Never
go near the bottle.*

Nobody had to tell me
that booze was a terrible way to die.

But this was a party,
and I was person for the very first time.

You won't know what I mean
unless you've been there too.
The bugs drowned till morning.

Say what you want about addiction.
I pulled the hair out of the drain with my hands.

I took it home.
I gave it a name.

CLOTHESLINES

Remembering Detroit; the 12th story window
of our hotel room. You pointed to the square
where the crowds would gather

their union signs in the 20 degree cold.
Gray coats, gray hair,
even on the young folks.
Each lifted voice, an engine

built to outlast any factory design.
You always said the word *Michigan*
like the sweetest prayer.

Driving through the back roads near Lansing
I knew you would murder anyone in the car
who made fun of the plastic deer lawn ornaments.

You taught me good taste
is respecting good people, who keep
the oven open in winter to fight
the overpriced cold.

We both believe good poems
should come with that kind of heat.

But yours can convince a room
full of 500 anarchist queers
to feed the plums of their hearts
to an old man who wakes at six every morning

and drives to the public school to watch
the janitor raise the American flag.

Everything I know about class
I learned from your lipstick color: *Red State.*

I still find it on my neck sometimes, pooling

near my collarbone. A lake as big as the ocean
without the tide to bring you back
to shore.

You were never sure about me.
You watched of all my pick-up lines drop things.

But I don't play that game anymore.
I spend all of my time learning

to bake casseroles in case the neighbors get sick.
And I've already hung all my secrets on the clothesline.
You can look out the window and see

the last time I lied through my teeth,
my jaw wouldn't let me sleep
for 6 months. My conscience buzzed
like one of those terrible mosquito killing zapper machines.

I've finally learned love
is a screened-in porch.
I've finally learned love
is knowing everybody's name
in the town of your reasons to run.

I've finally learned love prays
it won't always live paycheck to paycheck.
But it always does,

even when it's got forever on its lips.
Forever ago you gave me a doorknob
as a gift. I am still learning to be an open

road to the tree that can be climbed to safety.
I think we're both still learning to believe
the union can always win. Michigan,

we all have hearts that wanna be old pick-up trucks
permanently parked in someone's front yard.

I'm gonna keep fixing mine up and someday
you're gonna be sure as the sun

it's never gonna run.

LOVE'S WEIGHT

My mother would say
my grandma only went to church
for the brunch that followed

at the Wichachee Diner
where she'd order
Big Breakfast Number Two
with extra toast

and stop for a banana split
at the take-out window
of the corner store on her way home.

And that's to say
she was the type
to buy too much Halloween candy
and forget to leave the light on
for the trick-or-treaters.

I watched her do that every year

till her son Peter died,
and then her daughter Barbara too,
and I suppose a mother can't lose
two children and want

to take a bite out of anything
but god's invisible face.

The last time I saw her
she was in a rocking chair,
not rocking.

The doctor said she had
been refusing to eat for weeks.

I know some people could watch

someone die like that
without deciding love is nothing

but hunger for certain
and unlivable grief.
But I was not someone
who could do that.

And still, my love, and still, my love.

In 2008 I went on tour with Sonya Renee, a Black poet and activist, and the founder of The Body is Not an Apology. I started the tour naively thinking I had my white privilege in check, but was less than an hour into the month of shows when it was clear that I absolutely did not. We were doing a cross-country tour, performing at nearly 25 universities. As universities tend to be more privileged environments there were more nights than not when there wasn't a single Person of Color in the audience. Among the many things that I, as a white person, have had the luxury of never considering in my life, I had never considered what it might be like to stand on stage and pour my heart out night after night while rarely seeing a face in the audience that looked like mine. I had simply never thought about it before, like I had simply never thought about the countless other privileges I had spent a lifetime taking for granted, and would begin to unpack on that tour.

PRIVILEGE IS NEVER HAVING TO THINK ABOUT IT

She steps out of the hotel bathroom
stiletto sharp in all her glossy glossy,
dressed to the nines. Glittering
a bold burgundy neckline
with elegant tailored boom,
locks her shining eyes
on the worn t-shirt
I haven't changed in days
and says,

Are you gonna wear that on stage?

I smile, gloating in the cool of my gritty apathy,
the oh-so-thrift-store of my dirty grunge.
She says,

Honey, do you have any idea
how much privilege it takes
to think it's cool to dress poor?

You wear that dirty shirt and you're a radical
saving the world. I wear that dirty shirt
and I am a broke junkie thief
getting followed around every store.

That conversation happened years ago.
On the same tour where Sonya watched me
pay 75 bucks to have my hair cut
in way that would make me look,
"Like I can't afford a haircut."

The same tour that began the day after
I was the featured performer at a university's
Women of Color Symposium.
No, I did not ask why they weren't
featuring a Woman of Color instead.

Yes, I got paid.
I'm pretty sure it was a good paycheck.

I'm also pretty sure
someone got a good paycheck
when "Trayvon Martin Gun Range Targets"
sold out in 2 days.

I know those things are not exactly the same.

I know I wanted to burn every noose-white seam
of our cotton flag when Trayvon Martin's mother
was on the witness stand trying to convince
a jury of mostly white mothers that she could
recognize the sound of her own son's scream.

I know I wanted to split the fucking sky
when I heard that whip of a verdict
and Sonya posted online,

How many different ways can this country tell me I am worthless?

I know it was right then
that I walked upstairs
and started counting the hoodies
in my closet. There are 14 hoodies
in my closet that tell me my family

will never have to hear justice say
it wasn't till I was lying in my casket
that I was wearing the right clothes. I will never

be forced to dress
a wound as deep as my mother's heart.
She will never be woken in her sleep
to peel my body off gated grass,
to beg god to sew the sudden hole in my chest.

LENS

I've been practicing gratitude.
I've been skipping entire weeks.
Practicing a wider lens. Listening
for the bully's heartbeat
Hearing it in my own chest.

I've been remembering the time I cried
in a cloud of tear gas at a peaceful protest.
How I decided I was too soft to last,
and then I decided to be softer.

I've been remembering way way back
to the moment they told me Jesus walked on water.
How I knew whatever I'd grow up to believe

I would never try to wrestle a miracle
away from anyone's reason to live.
I've been remembering how I wrestled a miracle
away from your reason to live.

If only shame could wash me clean,
but that is never how healing works.
Nobody ever won anything from anyone
thinking the whole world was out of their league.
I'm sorry you know

what I look like when no one is looking.
I don't expect anyone to believe
in justice and forgiveness at the same time.

If it's any consolation
I feel like a ferris wheel in a snowbank
twenty years after they shut down the park.

If it's any consolation I've been living in my head
whenever anyone tells me I have a good heart.
And I think about you. I think about you.

PRISM★

My friend Derrick says, "Love
is the only war worth dying for."
But every time I say, *Please come back*
I feel the other war in me renewed.
The war of desperation. My trauma flag.

I suppose we wear our traumas
the way the guillotine wears gravity;
our lovers' necks are so soft.

I lost my head so many times
I got sober just hoping my eyes would dry;

still I drink so much in my sleep
I can't sleepwalk a straight line
to the guest room where collapse
hangs so heavy inside her lungs
she speaks and her voice trips across her heartbeat.
Each word limps into the air:

We are gone, she says.

And I am no mortician.
I have no idea how to put makeup on the dead.
I have no idea how to un-erase

so I just puddle at the door,
my face looking like a deck of falling cards,
like everything's been playing me.

We tried so hard.

But when I said, *Give me a ring*,
she thought I meant a call.

Now I haven't had her number
for 2 years. She has been saying,

How many times are we gonna
keep cutting these red flags
into Valentines?

All the wars we've fought
have turned our shine into rust;
now we can't touch each other's trust
without a tetanus shot.

We can't begin to remember
how we forgot

there is no shelter in the womb;
the heart forms long before the ribcage.
My mother swore she could feel me kicking
weeks before my feet formed.

That's how hard my heart beat.
And still does.

But they say the womb is where we learn love
is knowing the chord that feeds you
could at any moment wrap around your neck.

I hold my breath for the entire 56 seconds
it takes her to walk to the window,
to stare at the road
to tell me she has nothing left,
to tell me we are done

carrying our level heads
in our torn up chests.

And for the first time I know she is right

as the dawn after our first date.
We were so young

I hadn't written an honest love poem yet.

I hadn't met anyone I could fall so hard for
till the night we kissed on our skateboards.
She teased me for going so slow.

I said, *I never want to catch up
to the letting go.* I want the plead
in my throat to forever anchor my spine
in the seams of your warm slippers, love.

Even when that dove crashed through the window.
Even when our friends said, *You can call it love
but remember Einstein called himself a pacifist
when he built the bomb.*

When they ask me why we stayed together
for so long
I say, *I don't know.*

I just know we cried at the exact
same time in every movie.
I know we blushed everyday
for the first two years. I know
I always stole the covers and she never woke me up.

I know the exact look on her face
the first time she used my toothbrush.

The next day I brushed my teeth 40 some times
because I didn't want to let her go.

You have to understand
when it hurt to love her
it hurt the way the light hurts your eyes
in the middle of the night.
But I had to see, even through the ruin,
if what we were burying were seeds.

There were so many plants in our house
you could rake the leaves. Even through that winter

when I was trying to make angels
in the snow of her cold shoulder,
she was still leaving

love notes in my suitcase. I'd always find them
the day before I left. I remembered a story
her mother told me.
She said,

Andrea, when Heather was a little girl
she couldn't fall asleep without tying
a string around her finger
that she stretched to mine in the other room.
All night long she'd give that string the tiniest tug
to make sure I was still there.
And when I tugged back, that was love.
That was love.
As easy as that. Sometimes.

*"Love is the only war worth dying for." From *Born in the Year of the
Butterfly Knife* by Derrick Brown.

RIOT

Sometimes hope is a thing with feathers
flying away from the fight.

DURING THE WORST OF IT

During the worst of it
everything was radio static.
Everything was inching toward the bathtub.
I woke fevered and flailing
in a fit of my own ghost.

I forgot yesterday was yesterday.

Nothing was as honest as
the quiet
at the end of a scream.

My mind was an always flaring rash
and I was tearing through everyone I loved
to scratch the bloody wound of it.

I felt the bugs come,
chasing my sanity like a starved fire.

I got out of bed one morning
to pour a glass of water and discovered
the kitchen faucet was gone.
I thought it was

the creepy prank of someone who had snuck
into my house in the middle of the night.
Then I walked back into the kitchen
to find the faucet had never been missing.

My friend with the same disease
called it an "un-hallucination"
where you stop seeing things
that are right there.

She said for a while she had quit driving
because she had turned into traffic too many times
thinking the road was completely clear.

This is and isn't
what happened to our love.

I woke up one morning, pointed to your chest
and said, *Your heart has disappeared.*
You said, *No sweetheart. I promise, my heart*

is right here.

1988

It was the year your mother
put her cigarette out on your arm.
The year you forgave her so hard
you stopped crying for good.

I was on the other side of the world
watching my father shine his knives.
I was trying to get the nerve to tell him
who to kill.

But he never figured out
there was someone to kill.
Collected knives like art
and hung them on our walls.

That autumn I made a person
by stuffing a pile of dead leaves
into an old pair of clothes.
Maybe you did too. Maybe

you found a pumpkin for a head
and dug it hollow with your hands.

Friend, if memories had been seeds
we could have chosen not to plant
do you think we would have ever found each other?

Do you believe in the magnet of scars? I believe

people who have been through hell
will build their love from the still burning coals.

Our friendship is a well-heated home
where we always agree on what is art

and what is something to sharpen
and hold in our ready hands.

BALLAD OF THE UNUSED TANDEM BICYCLE

The boy-looking one:
I thought I could've done without those wimpy legs
and the tough-faced fear,
the one who never changes clothes,
who never locks me up.

The one who talks to himself for miles.
You'd think he was trying to build a fan base
of dust.

The one who got sick
and couldn't pedal me
for two years. Dust.

I just sat there
remembering the day they'd bought me, hoping
I could take both of them everywhere.

The boy-looking one,
who was always on the back seat
playing with the bell. He's the only one still here;

walks past me every day, like a church
given up on prayers.

When she left
he hardly noticed the red lights,
her absent tears.

I wish you could've seen
how their lungs could
turn a hard pedaled hill
into a year they'd won.

A year taken back.

Every time
they'd reach the top of the hill
the boy-looking one would press
his ear to the girl's spine, listen

for that moment when the saw of her breath
would cut down every tree
that had ever grown a ring
he hadn't shined for her hand.

This is where they'd sing,
my tassels twirling
in their tender threaded palms.

This is where
they'd ring the bell
and follow each other
to the salt of their lips,
where they'd blush new as strangers

and say, *Let this be the day*
we see start seeing what we saw
when we first met.

Let the hands of that reaper clock
unbury our fever,
our alleyway waltz,
our top down drive
up the California coast,
with the elephant seals
and Big Sur on fire.

The first time
we bought a shower curtain together.

That day was plenty, they'd say.
Give us back that kind of weather,
they'd say, the boy's face

still pressed against the girls spine.

The girl opened her arms and wore him like a crown,
smiling all the way down the hill, towards home.

The boy whispered, *Thank you for peddling me.*
I know how heavy I can be.

I miss those wimpy legs
and the girl with the redwood spine who smiled
like every leaf on every tree
was a new leaf turning over,
pedals losing their dust.

PLACE

Love is the place
where the wounded
started calling the wounds
on their knees *strawberries*.

PLUM

Sometimes I think
I could kill him.

Sometimes I think
I could walk into his home,
push past his lilied wife
and crack his neck over my knee-cap
like the first beat of a song.

Sometimes I can almost feel
his skull, softening to a plum
beneath my heel,

his cheekbones kicked to salt,
his fault, his fault, his fault
spilling out his ears.

Sometimes I get sick

of writing poems
about my fear,
about shame,
about hiding
the chafe marks from his beard

when I was swimming at the pool.

Sometimes
I don't want to write
anything but the line

that wraps around his neck.

FOR THE LEAVING

Nobody
ever thinks
about the weight
of a comet, how heavy
something has to be to go
that fast.

ORBIT

You were born 6 years before I was.
In that entire time, and a trillion years before that,
I was spinning up in space
all light and bliss and orbit,
no grief or hurt or bitterness, all poetry
and no language, not a single need
for words like *forgiveness*.

I was up there making snow angels
in the star dust
when I glanced down and saw you on a playground
shy as a comet, chewing on your hair.

I turned to the Milky Way and said
I found her. Get me down there.

The first time we were face to face
it was a Sunday in New Orleans.
Holy as you are, I'm pretty certain
you were high as a kite. And I wanted to be the key
tied the end of that string catching all of your electricity.

When I finally got the nerve to kiss you
we were in the Colorado desert
beneath the same night sky
you would point to months later and say, *Baby,
we could make any of those specks of light
the Big Dipper if we drew the lines right.*

I suppose it was all that possibility
that made us both so bad at actually knowing
where to draw the line.

Me, running down the street chasing your taxi,
crying at the top of my lungs. I mean
the absolute rooftop of my skyscraper lungs.

You, deboarding the airplane
with your suitcase still on it,
racing back home to find my faith
a burning piano.

I am so desperate to learn
how people reach each other
I can't stop running around
cursing this city for the day they started burying
the telephone wires underground.

Will we ever be easy?
Will we ever sleep like rocks
without worrying we will wake like volcanos?
We can be so explosive
I start thinking a good day is a slow burn.

But I never stop dreaming of the ocean
where the salt curled your hair,
how you blushed in your apron
when that radio show
on the stereo started making you cry.

I love you so much
your touch is the kind of mercy that quiets regret.
I know I will never stop wanting you
to spend forever painting your toenails in my bed.
Sweet skylight of a woman,
I know you're good in a storm.
I know you swam right back to New Orleans
the second the hurricane
had her reaching for your hand.

But you still deserve the sun,
and we still deserve the sun
and I don't want to write one more poem
about peace 'til I've figured out
how to sew a white flag out of our bed sheets.

So tonight, let me drive you
through the backroads of this country
to where the meadow lifts its lungs to the sky
and let me show you how the last two angels
I made in the stardust were you and I

and if we make it or if we don't,
I want you to know it was
absolutely worth it.

'Cause I might have learned the word *grief*
but I never learned the word *bitterness*

and I know all poetry is forgiveness
for what this world can not always hold.

Shy comet, chewing on your hair,
come see what's in the stars tonight.
Come hold my hand and let me
show you what is up there.

TRUCE

I was little.
My mother was a bank teller.
I called her a fortune teller.
She nicknamed me Pangee.
Not Pangea. I was never in one piece.

The first time I called someone ugly
I had an ice-cream headache
for 3 weeks. Tell that to my future.
Say, *The moon doesn't care to be a bully when it's full.*

I was running from myself on empty.
Not much made sense. For instance: the Russians didn't like us
because they couldn't afford blue jeans. What?

What I knew
is that I wasn't killing spiders 'cause I was scared of them.
I was killing them 'cause they were scared of me.

You can have a cold war with yourself
even in the summertime.

I watched the rocks get slapped by the sea.
I knew the sea was made of the same stuff as tears.
That meant if you were hurting
you could understand the sharks.
You maybe carried them between the ears.
You maybe heard the word *love*
and started running from the teeth.

I was running around with a panic in my chest.
The teacher said, *Silence is golden.*
I wanted to say, *Silence is bronze at best,*
but I'd already time-capsuled my voice box,
knowing someday I'd be either brave or scared enough
to dig it out and open it all the way up.
That's how I got here,

in this old rocking chair
typing with my grandma's thimbles on my fingers.
Every poem is a something being sewn.
Every poem is me asking,
Are we there yet? Are we there yet? Years
after they told me I was already home,
my love's feet were still not welcome on the welcome mat.
But you've never seen 2 bridges
that could arch like that

so we crossed the river to where the echo took us in.

That's how I learned bouncing back
is about being honest with the canyon.

That's how I got this see-through skin,
this glow-in-the-dark fear, this need to tell you,
I don't always have the best atmosphere.

I was not a child the last time
I threw a full tantrum fit in the grocery store.
I was not poor the last time I stole
someone's heart

like it wasn't worth my change.

I do not need air traffic control
to tell me there may never be enough flights
for me to lose all of my baggage. Still

I know a lot can shift
if I am willing to claim it
at the same carousel where I learn

BEATING YOURSELF UP IS NEVER A FAIR FIGHT.

It only knocks the wind out of your chances
to come clean through that canyon,

to be exactly who you are
so you might become
exactly who you want to be.

I want to write my entire life
using only the shift key.
I want to mess up, bounce back,

then let myself be the hinge
that keeps opening the door
to look myself straight in the eye
to say, *Pangee, you didn't come here
to write your heart out.*

You came to write it in.

BEFORE THE FEVER BROKE

I started whispering to my love in bed
     I said
Who knew illness
     would be the thing

that would teach me how to *fall*
     in love with time

how to walk
   hand in hand
     with the second hand
  of the clock
    I said *now*

even when I can't walk

   my mouth is running
full circle around the sun
        to tattle on god

I said
      god is kissing behind
   the bleachers of my spine

I said *pain isn't only pain*

it is a teacher
    who could have caught me
but *let me fall* instead

     let my blood red lips *learn*

how to kiss bitterness

     goodbye

I said

remember

all the years
    I wanted to die

     remember

all the years
    I collected the sand for the hour glass

from the edge of a cliff
    I said

now *look at my* wrist, strutting

 like a prisoner
       who is done doing time

Look at these brand new clothes

          I said   my pulse

  finally

    in a bow-tie

MY

My body
torn from me
like a tooth.
No tooth fairy.
No god. Only me
and my rage
waiting for my bite
to grow in.

TO MY LOVE ON THE DAY SHE DISCOVERED TUMBLR AND EVERY LOVE POEM I EVER WROTE TO EVERY WOMAN I LOVED BEFORE HER

It doesn't matter
that you may have a slight tendency
towards extreme jealousy.

It doesn't matter that you are one of five sisters
and I have often pictured you at two years old
ripping your mother's nipple out of your baby sister's mouth
and screaming, THAT'S MINE, MOTHERFUCKER!

It doesn't matter.

All of that aside,
I can't imagine it would be easy for anyone
to see it all out on the line, two decades of panties.
And it's not even that I got around. It's that I'm old
and I've written every fucking detail down.

Damnit, Tumblr, you tattling piece of shit.

Love, remember that time
I saw a photograph of your mortifyingly attractive ex
and suddenly my field of vision became a junkyard of vision?
Remember how I couldn't get my sanity to start?

I just kept running my mouth
about how I knew she was a better lover
because she lived in Oakland and worked at Trader Joe's.
(Fuck all of the hot people at Trader Joe's.)

I understand why you would not want
to hear every hungry promise

I have ever haikued into someone's ear
when that one photo had me

like a deer in the headlights
of the car where her backseat first wet its mouth
on the way you breathe the word *baby*.

But baby, I don't think either of us wants the truth
filed down and hidden from the guards.

My heart in your slingshot, I swear,
we had to be aiming perfectly
every love of the way to end up here.

Call every other lover *the air that carried us*.
A tailwind, every, *Do you think she likes me?* message
you ever forwarded to your best friend.

Every maybe breakup you chewed your knuckles for.
Every time you cried your makeup off in an airport
was you unfurling your ribbon heart,
a hundred red carpets on their way to me.

You never have to say you did not love hard.
I know you. I know you were all in.

I know you lit up like a Kansas runaway
spotting the Hollywood sign
every time you'd leave a room and overhear
their mothers whispering *I love her.*

Of course they did.
Keep every bit of that forever.
Call it a hundred poems that were holy true.
That we come to each other with all of their fire
inside of us, with all of that ruin and flutter,
every crushing first fight where you both cried all night
trying to gather the wine back into the grape.

Every holiday she was not welcome home
and you covered her apartment in Christmas lights.

All that tender and beg and surrender,
and every promise we broke
like bread to feed ourselves better,
to come here jealous and on fire and willing,

to hold each other through every moment
the past feels like a sword to swallow,
to say, *Finally finally finally, my love,*
you must know what I would have given
to have been beside you all along.

I have to wake up every day and forgive time
for teaching me how to waltz
before anyone had written my favorite song.

07/13/2013, JOURNAL ENTRY
George Zimmerman Found Not Guilty

Every unopened voice box is a closed casket.
The heavens are so full of hell
I can hear the stars playing taps
whenever I'm flying home.

What if the weather keeps changing
and we don't?

I want to touch the sleeve of the river.
I want to un-dam my bloodstream.
I want to make good time.

I don't know what makes us human
more than our crimes

and that just breaks me.

The last time I wanted to kill myself
my lover said she thought
I'd picked up the knife
to kill her instead.
I don't want to write that down.
But I don't want to keep it in my head.

There have been whole years
when I have been nothing but mean.
I want to leave behind my shame.
Cut all my words

from a shiny magazine. Sleep like a baby
so someone will hear me when I cry.

I want to be nothing but honest
and start saying nothing
but *it hurts, it hurts.*

My bare knuckled fear has hit
the road and left every single love
I have ever known.

So what do all these poems mean?

The war goes on.
I write it down and it's just as tall.

The war goes on
and I am small as a kid
being pushed inside of a locker.

Good god, I want to be big.
Big enough to stop
editing the ugly out of my bio.

To empty every bullet
from the chamber of my heart
and fill it with the hoodie of a boy.

What poem will walk him home?
What radio tower of light?

What redemption could dull
the blade, melt it down to mirror,
give us back to god?

Unhaunt the house
of the mother
choosing the color
of the casket.

Rinse out the mouth
of anyone
who stills calls it a white

flag. Tonight, don't tell me
you don't understand the kids

who cut themselves to save their lives,
who can't bare
to not be bleeding

when everything else is.

HONEY

She keeps her makeup in a ceramic bowl
of bullets beside a jelly jar full of gardenias
on an old dresser in Mississippi where outside
tomato plants grow in the bellies of old boats.

And she carries a knife
just in case she finds something
she wants to carve her name into.

I swear to god
if I had an adam's apple
I would tell her to peel it
and take a bite.
Meaning
this time

I'm not turning back.
I'm not turning in.
I'm turning over
every leaf of all my leaving.
I'm moonlighting as the moonlight.
My shine is working overtime
just to hear her call me *Honey*.
It makes me feel like
the bees' knees.

Like I could finally lose my past
like the keys to the getaway car.
Like all my fucking up
might finally be out of gas.

What if there will be no more war
fought in my name? What if
my name is nothing but *Honey*?

Do you realize I gave up on this in my twenties?
You were the first thing

I ever wrote on a vision board.
I cannot wait to tell you the truth
better than I have ever told the truth before.
And no, that does not mean I'm gonna
tell you you look like Marilyn Monroe,
but you do, and it makes me wanna run

for President. Jesus fucking Kennedy.

Do you know how gorgeous you are
when you're tripping? Literally tripping.
I have never met anyone more clumsy.
You walk into a room and turn every head
when you crash to the floor.

And I yell, *That's my girl!*
That is my girl!
And no, she's not embarrassed.
That's a sunburn she already had
from my moonlight.

I'm gonna trampoline
every inch of cement in this town,
and she's gonna teach me how to bounce back
mixing her southern polite
with her New Orleans *Fuck Off.*

I want to hear every story about your whole life.
Tell me again about your boombox birthday cake.
Tell me again how you're a master pumpkin carver.
Tell me again how you've never ever been to therapy.
Why does that turn me on?

You have a friend who
tattooed the words *You Wish*
on her ring finger.
I have a friend who
pulled out her tampon
on the streets of Manhattan

and threw it at a misogynist cop.

We are perfect for each other.

Come drink like a fish in my desert city.
I wanna be the fairy in your Irish pub.
I wanna be your pretty boy.

I want you to tell all your friends
you're out of my league
so I can slap you a high-five
when I'm sliding into home.

So when I start writing down our love
in public poems you know
you can burn all of my books
if I don't live up to my word.

If you ever have any doubt that I'm gonna live up
to the altitude of your highest hopes
remember

it was for you that I conquered my fear
of flying. For you that I learned
the ropes of Rescue Remedy:
do not under any circumstances
rip off the top of the bottle
and start chugging it like booze.
You'll freak out everyone on the plane,
and you don't want enemies at 30 thousand feet.

Trust me, Honey
you just need to know
this is the first time
I've ever done this
without looking for an exit row.
And I'm pretty certain my seat can't float
but I've already fallen out of the sky for you.
I've already said no to the parachute,

already told my mother:

you curse like a sailor
and you love like
the war is finally over
and you've just come home
and you are screaming my name
running down the dock in the harbor.
You're screaming *Honey, Honey!*
and I'm screaming *Don't trip!*
And you're screaming *Honey!*
and I'm screaming *Baby, don't fall down.*

I'm running for your red lips.
I'm running for your red heart
with my red heart red
as a Mississippi sunset.
Honey Honey Honey.

ACKNOWLEDGMENTS

Thank you Natalie Illum, for your tireless help in editing and your consistent willingness to tell me, "That line makes no sense, AT ALL." Thank you Emily Clay, for catching my tantrums in your bare hands. Thank you B Mann, for blessing the cover design with a photo of your stubborn pansy charm. Thank you Carolyn Suslovich, for inspiring "Royal Heart". Thank you Dr. Daniel Kinderlehrer, for opening the windows of my faith. Thank you Kelsey Gibb and Julia Seldin, for building StayHereWithMe.com into a community of wonderful light. Thank you to every person who has ever had a panic attack in public. Thank you to every person who keeps running towards and towards and towards. And finally, thank you to the word "heart" for making an appearance in just about every poem in this book, much to the dismay of my publisher and party man, Derrick Brown. I Heart you all. Hearts forever. Heart-On.

—andrea andrew gibby

ABOUT ANDREA GIBSON

Andrea Gibson is a queer/genderqueer poet and activist whose work deconstructs the current political machine, highlighting issues such as gender, sexuality, patriarchy, white supremacy, capitalism, classism, illness, love and spirituality. Gibson is a co-founder of Stay Here With Me, an online website and community focused on suicide prevention. Gibson has published three books, released six full length albums, and is the editor of WE WILL BE SHELTER, an anthology of social justice poetry, published by Write Bloody Publishing.

IF YOU LIKE ANDREA GIBSON, ANDREA LIKES...

Redhead and the Slaughter King
Megan Falley

What the Night Demands
Miles Walser

Write About an Empty Birdcage
Elaina Ellis

Racing Hummingbirds
Jeanann Verlee

Good Grief
Stevie Edwards

Write Bloody Publishing distributes and promotes great books of fiction, poetry and art every year. We are an independent press dedicated to quality literature and book design, with an office in Austin, TX.

Our employees are authors and artists so we call ourselves a family. Our design team comes from all over America: modern painters, photographers and rock album designers create book covers we're proud to be judged by.

We publish and promote 8-12 tour-savvy authors per year. We are grass-roots, D.I.Y., bootstrap believers. Pull up a good book and join the family. Support independent authors, artists and presses.

**Want to know more about Write Bloody books, authors, and events?
Join our mailing list at**

www.writebloody.com

WRITE BLOODY BOOKS

After the Witch Hunt — Megan Falley

Aim for the Head: An Anthology of Zombie Poetry — Rob Sturma, Editor

Amulet — Jason Bayani

Any Psalm You Want — Khary Jackson

Birthday Girl with Possum — Brendan Constantine

The Bones Below — Sierra DeMulder

Born in the Year of the Butterfly Knife — Derrick C. Brown

Bouquet of Red Flags — Taylor Mali

Bring Down the Chandeliers — Tara Hardy

Ceremony for the Choking Ghost — Karen Finneyfrock

Courage: Daring Poems for Gutsy Girls — Karen Finneyfrock, Mindy Nettifee
& Rachel McKibbens, Editors

Dear Future Boyfriend — Cristin O'Keefe Aptowicz

Dive: The Life and Fight of Reba Tutt — Hannah Safren

Drunks and Other Poems of Recovery — Jack McCarthy

The Elephant Engine High Dive Revival anthology

Everyone I Love Is a Stranger to Someone — Annelyse Gelman

Everything Is Everything — Cristin O'Keefe Aptowicz

The Feather Room — Anis Mojgani

Gentleman Practice — Buddy Wakefield

Glitter in the Blood: A Guide to Braver Writing — Mindy Nettifee

Good Grief — Stevie Edwards

The Good Things About America — Derrick Brown & Kevin Staniec, Editors

The Heart of a Comet — Pages D. Matam

Hot Teen Slut — Cristin O'Keefe Aptowicz

I Love Science! — Shanny Jean Maney

I Love You Is Back — Derrick C. Brown

The Importance of Being Ernest — Ernest Cline

In Search of Midnight — Mike McGee

The Incredible Sestina Anthology — Daniel Nester, Editor

Junkyard Ghost Revival anthology

Kissing Oscar Wilde — Jade Sylvan

The Last Time as We Are — Taylor Mali

Learn Then Burn — Tim Stafford & Derrick C. Brown, Editors

Learn Then Burn 2: This Time It's Personal— Tim Stafford, Editor

Learn Then Burn Teacher's Manual — Tim Stafford & Molly Meacham, Editors

Live for a Living — Buddy Wakefield

Love in a Time of Robot Apocalypse — David Perez

The Madness Vase — Andrea Gibson

Multiverse: An Anthology of Superhero Poetry of Superhuman Proportions — Rob Sturma & Rky Mcintyre, Editors

The New Clean — Jon Sands

New Shoes on a Dead Horse — Sierra DeMulder

No Matter the Wreckage — Sarah Kay

Oh, Terrible Youth — Cristin O'Keefe Aptowicz

Our Poison Horse — Derrick C. Brown

Over the Anvil We Stretch — Anis Mojgani

Pole Dancing to Gospel Hymns — Andrea Gibson

Racing Hummingbirds — Jeanann Verlee

Readhead and the Slaughter King — Megan Falley

Rise of the Trust Fall — Mindy Nettifee

Scandalabra — Derrick C. Brown

Slow Dance with Sasquatch — Jeremy Radin

The Smell of Good Mud — Lauren Zuniga

Songs from Under the River — Anis Mojgani

Spiking the Sucker Punch — Robbie Q. Telfer

Strange Light — Derrick C. Brown

These Are the Breaks — Idris Goodwin

Time Bomb Snooze Alarm — Bucky Sinister

The Undisputed Greatest Writer of All Time — Beau Sia

CPSIA information can be obtained
at www.ICGtesting.com
Printed in the USA
FSOW02n0051011116
26829FS